Word of the Week
36 Weeks of Focused Character Building

A RESOURCE BOOK FOR SCHOOL COUNSELORS AND CLASSROOM TEACHERS

Counseling with HEART, LLC.

Word of the Week: 36 Weeks of Focused Character Building
Text copyright 2014 Erainna Winnett
Cover Design Tony Loton
Interior Layout Carii Lu Designs

Library of Congress: Cataloging-in-Publication Data
Winnett, Erainna
Word of the Week: 36 Weeks of Focused Character Building
Summary: Resource book written to allow school counselors and educators the opportunity to teach character building throughout the school year.
1. Character Education—Education. 2. Social Skills and Aspects—Education
3. Morals and Values—Education 4. Interpersonal Relations—Education

ISBN-13: 978-0692225622
ISBN-10: 0692225625

CounselingwithHEART.com

Printed in the United States of America
10 9 8 7 6 5 4 3 2 1

WATCH YOUR THOUGHTS;
they become words.

WATCH YOUR WORDS;
they become actions.

WATCH YOUR ACTIONS;
they become habits.

WATCH YOUR HABITS;
they become character.

WATCH YOUR CHARACTER;
it becomes your destiny.

~Frank Outlaw

List of Character Traits and Behaviors

Attitude
Friendliness
Kindness
Fairness
Compassion
Caring
Honesty
Trustworthy
Cooperation
Motivation
Determination
Commitment
Positive self-talk
Self-Confidence
Self-esteem
Self-respect
Dedication
Courage

Generosity
Gratitude
Self-control
Self-reliance
Acceptance
Accountability
Courtesy
Empowerment
Forgiveness
Honorable
Initiative
Leadership
Motivation
Patience
Perseverance
Resilience
Respect
Sportsmanship

Table of Contents

Table of Contents *(Continued)*

Table of Contents (Continued)

WEEK ONE

Word of the Week:

Attitude

Definition: A way of thinking about a situation that is demonstrated by one's behavior.

 **Thought for the Week:** Having a positive attitude can make even the toughest situations bearable.

Class Activity:

Attitude Charades – Students will pick one of the following scenarios from a hat. One student will act out or perform the situation. The other students will guess the scenario and the performer's attitude. Then a second student will perform the same scenario with a different attitude. Students may do the performances in pairs.

Choices:
- You arrive to class and find out there is a surprise test.
- Your brother forgot to take out the trash, and now you have to do it.
- Your favorite video game is broken and can't be played.
- You tried out for a sports team and didn't make it.
- Your parent promised to take you to the beach this weekend, but has to work and can't.
- Your best friend's seat has been moved, and they no longer sit near you in class.

☐ Monday:

Write a dialogue between two characters, one with a positive attitude and one with a negative attitude, in which they discuss one of the following situations:

- Both characters have missed the bus and will be late for school.
- Both characters are worried about an upcoming test in one of their classes.
- Both characters have been invited to a birthday party for someone they don't know well.

☐ Tuesday:

Write a paragraph about a time when either you or someone you know had to deal with a challenging situation and didn't have a positive attitude about it. What was the outcome? What could you, or the person you know, have done differently?

☐ Wednesday:

Respond to this prompt:
Even though I don't like to _____ (fill in with an activity or chore you don't enjoy), this week I am going to change my attitude by _____ (what you will do differently). Elaborate in a few sentences about the change you plan to make.

☐ Thursday:

Basketball player Michael Jordan once said, "A good attitude can turn a weakness into a strength." Do you agree with this statement? Explain your opinion in a few sentences.

☐ Friday:

Reflection – Reflect on this week's character study by responding to the following:
This week I changed my attitude by _____ (explain what change you made), and the result was _____ (explain what changed as a result).

WEEK TWO

Word of the Week:

Friendliness

Definition: Showing kindness toward another person.

 **Thought for the Week:** Be friendly to everyone; those who you think deserve it the least sometimes need it the most.

Class Activity:
Explain to students that one way to be friendly is to pay people sincere compliments. A sincere compliment is one that the other person believes. For example, if someone does poorly on a spelling test, it might not seem sincere to compliment his or her spelling.

Put all students' names into a basket and have each student pull one name. Students will spend five minutes talking to the person whose name they have drawn. Then they'll return to their desks and write a short note about the conversation, including offering a sincere compliment. When they've finished writing, they'll deliver the note to the other person.

(This is an opportunity to practice friendly letters.)

□ Monday:

Write a descriptive paragraph. Describe how your body language, facial expressions, and other nonverbal mannerisms tell others you are a friendly person. Use sensory details and imagery to bring your description to life.

□ Tuesday:

Friendly people pay attention to others when working in groups or having conversations. Make a list of things people sometimes do when talking to others that can seem unfriendly. Choose three items from your list and provide advice on how to avoid doing these things.

For example, it is rude to stare at your phone while talking with someone. How could someone break that habit and be a friendly person?

□ Wednesday:

Friendly people greet others, make eye contact, and smile. Write about an opportunity you have each day to be friendly to someone you don't know well, even if it's just by smiling. Who is the person? Where or when do you see him or her? What could you do to be friendlier to that person?

□ Thursday:

One way to be friendly is to invite people to join you in activities or be part of activities you enjoy with others. For example, you could invite someone to join you and your friends during lunch, in a game during recess, or for an after-school activity.

Write a letter inviting someone to join you, or you and your other friends, in some sort of activity.

□ Friday:

Reflection – Reflect on this week's character study by responding to the following: This week I made an effort to be friendlier to others, and the result was

_____.

WEEK THREE

Word of the Week:

Kindness

Definition: The quality of being friendly and considerate.

 **Thought for the Week:** No act of kindness, no matter how small, is ever wasted.

Class Activity:

Share with students about David Jamilly, who founded an annual Kindness Day in England to encourage people to focus on being kind to one another. Have students plan a kindness day in your classroom and choose one or more of the following activities, as well some they develop on their own, to celebrate being kind:

- Writing anonymous notes of encouragement to leave in the desks or lockers of other students
- Attending a school sporting team and cheering on every player by name
- Starting a class log of acts of kindness. Encourage students to contribute every day by sharing an act of kindness they performed.

☐ Monday:

One way to practice kindness is to focus on the positive and help uplift others. Make a list of five good things that have happened today. Share your list with a partner.

☐ Tuesday:

Gossiping or saying mean things about others is unkind. What can you do to encourage kindness when you hear others gossiping about someone?

☐ Wednesday:

When was the last time someone was kind to you? What did that person say or do that was generous or thoughtful? Write about what it felt like to receive an act of kindness.

☐ Thursday:

Kind people are generous. That doesn't mean you have to give money to others. You can be generous with your time or your words. Do you have an opportunity to make someone else's day easier or happier? Write about a simple way you can give of yourself to help someone else have a better day.

☐ Friday:

Reflection – Reflect on this week's character study by responding to the following:

> *Kind people do these things on a regular basis: (Make an elaborated list of three to five characteristics of kind people.)*

WEEK FOUR

Word of the Week:

Fairness

Definition: A situation in which everyone has the same opportunity, must meet the same expectations, or receives the same rewards for the same work or effort.

 **Thought for the Week:** "Win or lose, do it fairly." Knute Rockne)

Class Activity:

Ask students to think about whether there are situations in which fair does not mean equal. For example, if someone has a disability that makes it difficult to walk or run, is it fair that he or she has to run a mile to pass a physical education class? With a partner, have students brainstorm situations in which fair does not mean equal. Then ask them to explain how people can be given the same opportunities in different ways.

☐ Monday:

Complete the following prompt with a well-developed paragraph:
I am treated fairly when...

☐ Tuesday:

Write about a situation you or someone close to you experienced
that you felt was unfair. How could the situation have been
changed to make it fairer?

☐ Wednesday:

Fairness relies on the idea that everyone should be treated
equally and is entitled to the same things. Complete the
following writing prompt:

Everyone deserves...

☐ Thursday:

What happens when people are not treated fairly? What, for example, would
happen if grades were not fairly based on student achievement but rather on
how much a teacher liked a student? Write about the consequences of this or
another situation in which people were not treated fairly.

☐ Friday:

Rules and laws are one way society ensures that everyone is treated fairly. Think
of one rule in your school and write about how that rule ensures that every
student receives fair treatment.

WEEK FIVE

Word of the Week:

Compassion

Definition: Feeling or showing sympathy and concern for others.

 **Thought for the Week:** Being compassionate improves your own life and the lives of others.

Class Activity:
Explain to students that developing a school community that values compassion for others has many benefits. As a class, make a list of social problems that everyone feels are present in your school. Are there bullies? Do some people feel left out of activities? Once the list has several items, have students brainstorm acts of compassion that could help solve these problems.

☐ Monday:

Write a definition paragraph. Look up the word compassion. In your own words, write a definition based on what you've read. Then expand your response into a full paragraph using examples to illustrate what it means to be compassionate.

☐ Tuesday:

One way to be more compassionate is to find ways that you and others share experiences and challenges. Choose one of the following prompts and write about one way that you are like someone else you know. Write a complete paragraph that includes details about the similarities between you and another person.

Just like me, _____ (name) sometimes makes mistakes.

☐ Wednesday:

One way to build a compassionate outlook is to perform what some people call "random acts of kindness." Some examples of random acts of kindness might include shoveling a driveway for an older neighbor after a snowstorm or offering to help a stranger with his or her groceries in a parking lot. Think about the places you go in a normal week and the people you encounter. Write about an opportunity you have to commit a random act of kindness. After you've written about it, follow through and do something kind for another person.

☐ Thursday:

A step to developing a compassionate outlook is learning to forgive. Think of a time when someone did something that you felt was unfair or even unkind. What might have motivated that person to act in that way? Can you put yourself in the other person's shoes and forgive the person for what happened? Write about how you've reimagined the situation and found a path to forgiving the person.

☐ Friday:

Reflection – Reflect on this week's character study by responding to the following:

Make a list of five ways you can show compassion in your daily life.

WEEK SIX

Word of the Week:

Caring

Definition: Showing concern for the well-being and happiness of others.

 **Thought for the Week:** Sometimes all it takes is to show you care to become someone's hero.

Class Activity:
Share with students that caring people consider how they can help improve the lives of other people. As a class, choose one of the following activities:

- Have students write letters to a serviceman or servicewoman who is stationed in another country. In the letters, students will thank the soldier for his or her service and let him or her know that the class appreciates the soldier's sacrifice in being away from home.
- Having a caring attitude can benefit everyone in the school. As a class, have students make posters or flyers to hang around the school that offer single tips on how to be more caring. (For example, a poster might have a picture of one person holding open a door for someone instead of letting it slam shut.)
- If your school allows it, plan a "field trip" to a younger grade. Have students spend a few minutes chatting with individual students and asking them about what they like. Then students will write short notes to their younger student partners thanking them for taking the time to visit.

□ Monday:

Write a definition paragraph. Having a caring attitude often comes from having empathy for others. Look up the definition of the word empathy and write a paragraph explaining what it means. Use examples to demonstrate the main points in your definition. Use the dictionary as a reference, but write in your own words.

□ Tuesday:

Caring people think about how their actions might affect others. For example, if you borrow someone's pencil and don't return it, how could that affect that person later on?

Consider one of the following situations. Write a paragraph about how the action described could affect others, what that effect might be, and what change in behavior would result in a more caring approach.

- Your parent has asked you to take out the trash, but instead you go to your room and play a video game.
- You promised to help your sister with her homework, but you decided to watch your favorite television show first.
- You accepted an invitation to a classmate's birthday party but decide not to attend at the last minute.
- You agreed to meet a neighbor at the park on Saturday but woke up late and missed the meeting time.

□ Wednesday:

Caring people appreciate the other people in their lives. Consider the people in your life who care about you and show that they care through their words and actions. Write a thank-you note to someone in your life whom you really appreciate. Thank that person for something specific he or she has done, as well as for the general care he or she has shown you.

□ Thursday:

Caring people are polite. That doesn't mean you have to have very formal manners; rather, it means you treat those around you with respect. Make a list of five ways you are polite in your daily life. Then choose one and write a paragraph explaining how your good manners might make another person feel.

□ Friday:

Reflection – Reflect on this week's character study by responding to the following in at least one paragraph:

This week I identified three different ways that I am caring toward others.

WEEK SEVEN

Word of the Week:

Honesty

Definition: Truthfulness

 **Thought for the Week:** It is much easier to be honest than to keep track of lies.

Class Activity:
Share with students that there are many sayings and proverbs about honesty. In pairs, have students use the Internet or another resource to find a saying or proverb about honesty. Then have them make posters illustrating their saying to hang in the classroom or school.

☐ Monday:

Write a definition paragraph. Honesty is a familiar word, but it can mean different things to different people. Use a dictionary to find the definition of honest. Then write a paragraph to explain your own definition of the word.

☐ Tuesday:

A friend has broken a rule and is afraid she will get in trouble. Write a dialogue or short play in which you convince her to be honest about what happened.

☐ Wednesday:

Sometimes being completely honest can hurt someone's feelings. In a paragraph, explain why it is important to be kind when you are being honest.

☐ Thursday:

We count on some people in our lives to be honest with us at all times. Who is one such person in your life, and why is it important that the person be honest?

☐ Friday:

Reflection – Reflect on this week's character study by responding to the following in at least one paragraph:

This week, I considered the importance of honesty in different situations.

WEEK EIGHT

Word of the Week:

Trustworthy

Definition: Able to be relied upon to be honest.

 **Thought for the Week:** If a friend is not trustworthy, he or she is not a true friend.

Class Activity:

Explain to students that there are many benefits to being a trustworthy person. As a class, brainstorm a list of good consequences that come from being trustworthy. Then, in pairs, have students choose one consequence and write a story about someone who is trustworthy and is rewarded with that consequence.

☐ Monday:

Write a definition paragraph. You've written about what it means to be honest. Is being honest the same as being trustworthy? Explain how being trustworthy is similar to or different from being honest.

☐ Tuesday:

There are people in society we all count on to be trustworthy. Who is one of those people, and why is trustworthiness so important?

☐ Wednesday:

Sometimes people make mistakes. If a person is dishonest once, does that mean the person is no longer trustworthy? Why or why not?

☐ Thursday:

Is there a difference between being responsible and being trustworthy? Explain.

☐ Friday:

Reflection – Reflect on this week's character study by responding to the following in at least one paragraph:

Do you feel you are a trustworthy person? Why or why not?

WEEK NINE

Word of the Week:

Cooperation

Definition: The process of many people working together toward a single goal.

Thought for the Week: Competition can be valuable, but the most difficult problems can only be solved through cooperation.

Class Activity:

Using a rope, make a circle on the classroom floor. Students will work together so that everyone can sit down within the circle. Make the circle smaller so that students must cooperate in order to find a way for everyone to fit within the boundary.

After you have shrunk the circle two or three times, students will share the challenges they faced trying to get everyone into the circle and explain how they cooperated to make it work.

☐ Monday:

What is the difference between cooperation and competition? Explain your answer.

☐ Tuesday:

One of the benefits of cooperating with others is that you can sometimes form friendships with those on the same team or in the same group. Explain why cooperation often leads to friendship.

☐ Wednesday:

Describe a situation in which it is absolutely necessary for two or more people to cooperate. What would happen if the people in the group stopped cooperating?

☐ Thursday:

Write a dialogue or short play in which one character explains to another why it is important to cooperate with others. Use one of the following scenarios:
- Two people on the same sports team
- Two people who are planning a party
- Two people who are trying to assemble a puzzle

☐ Friday:

Reflection – Reflect on this week's character study by responding to the following in at least one paragraph:

It is important to cooperate when working with others because…

WEEK TEN

Word of the Week:

Motivation

Definition: A willingness to do one's best work.

 **Thought for the Week:** It all comes down to motivation. If you want to achieve something, you will work hard to do so.

Class Activity:

Motivation Museum – As a class, take a tour of the posters that students make on Thursday. Have each student choose two other students and read their posters carefully. Then have students write a note of encouragement to each of those students to help him or her stay motivated.

☐ Monday:

Definition – Look up motive in the dictionary and read the definition. Then, based on your understanding of the root word, write your own definition of motivation.

☐ Tuesday:

People who have personal goals are usually motivated to achieve them. What are your personal goals? Make a list of five things you'd like to accomplish in the future. Use details to explain each goal so that others can read and understand them.

☐ Wednesday:

Pick one of the goals you listed on Tuesday. Write a paragraph about being motivated to achieve that goal and the steps you are taking now to reach it.

☐ Thursday:

One way to help yourself stay motivated to achieve a goal is to commit publicly to it. That is, if you tell others about your goal, you might feel more motivated to achieve it. Draw a poster that illustrates your goal and why you are motivated to achieve it.

☐ Friday:

Reflection – Reflect on this week's character study by responding to the following in at least one paragraph:

It is important to have motivation because…

WEEK ELEVEN

Word of the Week:

Determination

Definition: A quality that leads a person to continue to do something, even if it's difficult.

 **Thought for the Week:** A dream doesn't become a reality through magic; it takes determination.

Class Activity:
Divide students into groups of two to four. Give each group a pack of playing cards. Assign each group the goal of building a house of cards at least four layers or stories tall (you may have to provide photos or directions). Tell students that they are to encourage each other and show determination in meeting the goal. After the activity, ask students to reflect and share on the problems they encountered and how their determination to complete the task helped them overcome those problems.

□ Monday:

Write a definition paragraph. Look up the word determination in the dictionary. Read the definition carefully and then write your own explanation of what it means to have determination. Use examples from your own life or elsewhere to elaborate.

□ Tuesday:

Having determination means you know what you want to accomplish and that you will not give up if you encounter a problem on your way to accomplishing that goal. What is something you would like to accomplish? What problem might you encounter as you try to achieve that goal?

□ Wednesday:

Review the goal you wrote about on Tuesday and the problem you identified as something that might get in the way of accomplishing that goal. In a paragraph, explain how you could overcome that problem and why you will need determination to do so.

□ Thursday:

What is something you are good at? Is it a sport? Playing an instrument? Playing a video game? How did you become so good at this activity? Write a paragraph about a time when you needed determination to become good at something you excel at.

□ Friday:

Reflection – Reflect on this week's character study by responding to the following in at least one paragraph:

To achieve my goals, I must have determination because…

WEEK TWELVE

Word of the Week:

Commitment

Definition: An attitude that involves working very hard to accomplish something or support someone.

 **Thought for the Week:** Unless you make a commitment, you have a dream or a promise but not a plan to achieve your goal.

Class Activity:

Working in pairs and using school resources for research, students will write a short presentation about a person who has achieved success through commitment. The presentation should include an illustration or poster as well as a short explanation to be read in front of the class. Students will present to the group.

Potential topics might include:
- Olympic athletes
- Scientists who have made important discoveries
- Political leaders
- Humanitarians

☐ Monday:

Write a definition paragraph. Look up the word commitment in the dictionary. Read the definition carefully. Then write your own explanation of what it means to be committed to a goal. Use examples from your own life or elsewhere to elaborate.

☐ Tuesday:

Coaches of sports teams often talk to players about the importance of commitment to the team. Now that you have an explanation of the meaning of commitment, explain in a paragraph why it is so important that players be committed to their team's success, even when they are not personally successful.

☐ Wednesday:

Many children have pets, and many others would like to have pets. As you may know, taking care of a pet requires commitment. In a short paragraph, explain why it is so important for someone to make a commitment to the well-being of an animal before adopting a pet.

☐ Thursday:

What is the difference between hoping you'll achieve a goal and making a commitment to achieve that goal? Write a paragraph explaining what changes when you move from a hope to a commitment.

☐ Friday:

Reflection – Reflect on this week's character study by responding to the following in at least one paragraph:

It is important to make a commitment to a goal or responsibility because...

WEEK THIRTEEN

Word of the Week:

Positive Self-Talk

Definition: Positive self-talk is what a person tells him- or herself that helps the person develop and maintain an optimistic point of view.

 **Thought for the Week:** Positive self-talk will help you look on the bright side of almost any situation.

Class Activity:
Explain to students that it can be challenging to think of an affirmation that will help them get started with positive self-talk. For this activity, students will choose a classmate and identify a positive trait about that student to help him or her get started. Then each student will create one to three affirmations for that classmate. Students will then practice saying their affirmations out loud.

☐ Monday:

The first step to developing positive self-talk is to get rid of the negative messages you give yourself every day. Make a list of negative thoughts you've had about yourself recently. Then pick a couple of them and write a few words about why each negative thought is not accurate.

☐ Tuesday:

One way to develop the habit of positive self-talk is to start with a few positive affirmations. Think of three things you would like to have happen. They could be things like "I will score a home run at the baseball game today" or "I will study enough to earn an A on my spelling test." Write down these affirmations and make a commitment to repeat them to yourself at least three times a day.

☐ Wednesday:

Research has shown that positive self-talk is effective in helping people overcome hardships and achieve their goals. Why do you think this is the case? Write a paragraph to explain why you think positive self-talk is effective.

☐ Thursday:

It can be challenging to overcome the habit of giving yourself negative messages about yourself, your abilities, your appearance, and so on. What can you do when you recognize that you're allowing negative thoughts to dominate? Explain how you can change your outlook and provide yourself with positive self-talk.

☐ Friday:

Reflection – Reflect on this week's character study by responding to the following in at least one paragraph:

Positive self-talk will help me be more successful because…

WEEK FOURTEEN

Word of the Week:

Self-confidence

Definition: A feeling of trust in your own abilities or qualities.

 **Thought for the Week:** "One important key to success is self-confidence. An important key to self-confidence is preparation." (Arthur Ashe)

Class Activity:
Share with the class that they are part of a group of students with a wide range of skills and abilities, and each one of them is an important part of the group. With your help, have students brainstorm a list of the wonderful attributes, skills, and abilities of people in the class. Then have students write a short paragraph that begins with "Our class is amazing because…"

☐ Monday:

To become more self-confident, you must first identify your own strengths. Write a paragraph explaining what is amazing about you. Don't be embarrassed or try to be modest. The paragraph should celebrate everything you love about yourself. You will not be asked to share with the class, so be as positive as you can.

☐ Tuesday:

Self-confident people take action and act in positive ways. Think of a situation you wish were different. For example, perhaps you don't like that you have to go to bed at 9:00. Write about how you can take positive action to try to change that situation.

☐ Wednesday:

To procrastinate is to put off something that needs to be done. Procrastination can wear down your self-confidence, as you always have that chore or responsibility waiting in the wings. What is something you procrastinate about doing? Write about how you're going to take positive action to resolve that procrastination and how doing so will help you improve your self- confidence.

☐ Thursday:

What are some reasons you don't feel confident about yourself? Do you worry about your hairstyle? The clothes you're wearing? That you wear braces? One way to overcome these hurdles to being more self-confident is to recognize that you are not the only person who has these concerns. Write about one thing you feel keeps you from being more confident. Then explain how other people have to deal with this same situation.

☐ Friday:

Reflection – Reflect on this week's character study by responding to the following in at least one paragraph:

To become more self-confident, I will…

WEEK FIFTEEN

Word of the Week:

Self-esteem

Definition: Confidence in one's own abilities.

 **Thought for the Week:** Self-esteem comes from learning to be your own best friend.

Class Activity:
Share with students that receiving external compliments can boost their self-esteem. Have students make a list of three or four open-ended questions such as "What do you like about me?" and "What am I good at?" Students should put their name at the top of their paper. Then students will pass around their papers, answering the questions for their classmates until time is called. When the sheets are returned to students, they will summarize the external compliments they've received.

☐ Monday:

Read the thought for the week. What does it mean to be your own best friend? What qualities would you expect from a best friend? Do you demonstrate those traits when you think about yourself?

☐ Tuesday:

Write a narrative about the person you want to be. Writing about yourself in the third person, describe your ideal version of you. For example, you might begin by writing "Mary is a thoughtful person who cares about her family and friends…"

☐ Wednesday:

Being successful helps build your self-esteem. What are you good at? What happens when you do something that you're good at? Write about a time when you succeeded—in school, in sports, playing a game with friends, or in any other situation— and explain how that made you feel.

☐ Thursday:

Comparing yourself to others can lower your self-esteem. No two people are completely alike, not even twins. What can you do the next time you find yourself making comparisons between yourself and others? How can you avoid making comparisons that are damaging to your self-esteem?

☐ Friday:

Reflection – Reflect on this week's character study by responding to the following in at least one paragraph:

To build my self-esteem, I can…

WEEK SIXTEEN

Word of the Week:

Self-respect

Definition: Liking oneself for who one is, not because of what one can do or accomplish.

 **Thought for the Week:** "When you are content to be simply yourself, and don't compare or compete, everyone will respect you." (Lao-Tzu)

Class Activity:

Self-Collages – Using pictures from magazines, newspapers, or the Internet, students will create collages that celebrate their values and definitions of themselves. Hang the collages around the room. Then have students walk around the room and try to guess which collage belongs to each student. You can number the collages or have students place sticky notes with their names next to the collages. Students may or may not choose to reveal which collage they made.

After the activity, ask students to write a brief reflection on whether they feel their outward personality reflects their personal values. Then they will comment on how being themselves outwardly can help them develop self-respect.

☐ Monday:

Read the thought for the week. How do you define yourself without comparing yourself to others? What are the attributes that make you, you, despite what others around you may do, say, or accomplish?

☐ Tuesday:

People with self-respect often have strong values or a strong sense of right and wrong. What are your values? What do you think is the most important personal attribute a person can have?

☐ Wednesday:

To build and maintain your self-respect, it is important to spend time with people who respect you. How can you tell if another person has respect for you? In a paragraph, explain the behaviors you can identify in people who have respect for you.

☐ Thursday:

An important aspect of self-respect is taking responsibility for your actions. People make mistakes, and no one is perfect. Think about a time when you made a mistake—it could be a behavior mistake in the classroom, something that happened at home, or something else. Did you take responsibility for your actions? If yes, how? If you're not sure, now that you look back at that time, what do you think you could have done differently?

☐ Friday:

Reflection – Reflect on this week's character study by responding to the following in at least one paragraph:

It is important to have self-respect because…

WEEK SEVENTEEN

Word of the Week:

Dedication

Definition: A feeling of loyalty or commitment to something or someone.

 **Thought for the Week:** "There are no shortcuts to anyplace worth going." (Beverly Sills)

Class Activity:

Olympic Dedication – Explain to students that while they may all be familiar with some of the stars of the recent Olympic Games, many athletes never become celebrities and live relatively normal lives except for their exceptional dedication to their sport. Write the list of lesser-known Olympic events below on the board. In pairs, have students choose one of the events and research one person who, through dedication, has become successful in this event. Then have students create a poster and a short presentation about the athlete and his or her dedication. Students will present their work to the class. In their presentations, they will summarize what they've learned about dedication from their research.

- Badminton
- Water polo
- Fencing
- Dressage
- Racewalking
- Trampoline
- Curling
- Handball
- Canoeing

☐ Monday:

Read the thought for the week. How is Ms. Sills' quote related to the definition of dedication? What sort of loyalty or commitment is she referring to?

☐ Tuesday:

One does not instantly become dedicated to a goal. It usually takes time and practice to build a habit of working hard to achieve a goal. What is a goal you have that will require hard work and dedication? What is the first step you can take to be dedicated to achieving that goal?

☐ Wednesday:

Humans are error-prone. We all make mistakes. If you skip doing something for one day, or even for one week, it doesn't mean you are no longer dedicated. For example, you could be a dedicated student who forgets about a test. How do you recover from a mistake and renew your dedication to a goal?

☐ Thursday:

Many people throughout history have made important changes to society due to their dedication to public service, social justice, or another goal. Who is someone from history or in the present whom you feel is dedicated to serving his or her community? What has that person done or said that leads you to make that conclusion?

☐ Friday:

Reflection – Reflect on this week's character study by responding to the following in at least one paragraph:

I am or plan to become dedicated to the personal goal of…

WEEK EIGHTEEN

Word of the Week:

Definition: The ability to do something one knows is difficult or dangerous.

 **Thought for the Week:** "It takes a great deal of courage to stand up to our enemies, but just as much to stand up to our friends." (J.K. Rowling)

Class Activity:

In pairs, have students review the following list of situations. Then have them choose one of the situations and draw a poster that illustrates the courageous choice one would make in this situation. Hang the posters around the room and ask students to discuss whether they agree or disagree on which is the more courageous choice.

- Fighting or walking away from a fight
- Being a bully or standing up for someone who is being bullied
- Ignoring a new student or making friends with a new student
- Following the crowd or doing something different on your own
- Quitting a task that is very challenging or trying to work hard and finish it
- Accepting responsibility for a mistake or trying to blame someone else

☐ Monday:
Read the thought for the week. What did J.K. Rowling mean? Why might it be difficult to stand up to your friends?

☐ Tuesday:
Is peer pressure a strong influence in this school? Does it take courage to resist peer pressure? Write about the effects of peer pressure and why one must show courage to stand up and be independent of it.

☐ Wednesday:
Is courage something one is born with? Can you develop courage as you grow older? Explain one step a person can take to become more courageous.

☐ Thursday:
Think of someone from history who has shown courage. Some examples might include Martin Luther King Jr., Susan B. Anthony, Rosa Parks, or anyone else who comes to mind. What did that person do that was courageous? What fears might he or she have had to overcome to be successful?

☐ Friday:
Reflection – Reflect on this week's character study by responding to the following in at least one paragraph:

> *One courageous thing someone might do is...*

WEEK NINETEEN

Word of the Week:

Generosity

Definition: The habit of giving without expecting anything in return.

 **Thought for the Week:** You can't live a perfect day without doing something for someone who will never be able to repay you.

Class Activity:

As a group, brainstorm a class project that will encourage every student to be more generous. Begin by making a list of organizations or groups that could benefit from the class's generosity. The list might include homeless shelters, animal shelters, nursing homes, and so on. Once students have identified a place or group they'd like to help with their generosity, identify for students what the organization needs (such as food, blankets, or pet supplies). Then, as a class, think of a way to collect these items to donate to the organization. When the project is finished, have each student write a short paragraph about how the class's generosity helped the organization or group.

□ Monday:
Read the thought for the week. What sorts of things can you do every day for others, without any expectation of being repaid?

□ Tuesday:
Sometimes people make the mistake of believing that the only way to be generous is by sharing money. In what way can you or others show generosity that doesn't involve money?

□ Wednesday:
Along with being generous, it is important to recognize the generosity of others. Think of a good deed that someone has done for you recently. Write a thank-you note to that person thanking him or her for being generous to you.

□ Thursday:
Write a dialogue or short play with at least two characters in which one character explains to the other character what it means to be generous. Make the play interesting by having the characters ask questions or disagree on what it means to be generous.

□ Friday:
Reflection – Reflect on this week's character study by responding to the following in at least one paragraph:

It is important that members of a community be generous because…

WEEK TWENTY

Word of the Week:

Gratitude

Definition: Being thankful.

 **Thought for the Week:** "Feeling gratitude and not expressing it is like wrapping a present and not giving it." (William Arthur Ward)

Class Activity:

Gratitude Book – Create a gratitude book to send home with a different child each week (or every few days). Each student will add a page of pictures, quotes, and drawings to explain what he or she, as well as his or her family, is grateful for. Once everyone has had a turn, share the book as a class and celebrate all the different reasons there are to be grateful.

☐ Monday:

Read the thought for the week. What does Mr. Ward mean? What happens to a gift that is wrapped and not given? How is that situation like not expressing your gratitude?

☐ Tuesday:

Think of something you are grateful for. Now imagine that what you are grateful for is a gift that was given to you. Write a thank-you note to the person you feel is responsible for you having this thing or experience.

☐ Wednesday:

Write a list of three good things in your life. Choose one and elaborate on why you appreciate that aspect of your life and how you are grateful for it.

☐ Thursday:

Using the Internet or another research source, find a quote about gratitude. Explain what it means in your own words and how it can be applied to your life.

☐ Friday:

Reflection – Reflect on this week's character study by responding to the following in at least one paragraph:

It is important to show gratitude for the good things in our lives because...

WEEK TWENTY-ONE

Word of the Week:

Self-control

Definition: The ability to manage one's own emotions, especially in difficult situations.

 **Thought for the Week:** "To handle yourself, use your mind; to handle others, use your heart." (Eleanor Roosevelt)

Class Activity:

Red Light/Green Light – This classic game is a wonderful way for students to practice self-control. Students can stand next to their desks. When you say "Green Light," students walk forward. When you say "Red Light," students must stop. Those who don't stop are "out" and must sit down. The first student to reach the front of the room wins. Change from "green light" to "red light" very abruptly so students who dart or lunge will not be likely to win. When the game ends, students will write a brief reflection on why they were or were not successful in the game.

☐ Monday:

Read the thought for the week. What does it mean to manage your emotions? Write an example of a time when you have managed your emotions.

☐ Tuesday:

Everyone has the experience of feeling upset or even angry. Sometimes people make bad choices when they are upset. Write about one way you use self-control to choose your actions more effectively when you are upset.

☐ Wednesday:

It is important to recognize what we and others look like when we are experiencing different emotions. Draw two pictures— one of someone who is happy and one of someone who is very angry. Beneath each face, write a list of characteristics you might observe in the person.

☐ Thursday:

Sometimes it is difficult to understand how a challenging problem can be solved, and it can be easy to become angry or to act without thinking about the consequences of an action. What are three steps a person should take when facing a challenging problem?

☐ Friday:

Reflection – Reflect on this week's character study by responding to the following in at least one paragraph:

It's important to have self-control because…

WEEK TWENTY-TWO

Word of the Week:

Self-reliance

Definition: The ability to depend on yourself to get things done and meet your own needs.

 **Thought for the Week:** "You cannot help people permanently by doing for them, what they could and should do for themselves." (Abraham Lincoln)

Class Activity:
Explain to students that young people learn to do new things at different times. Self-reliance is very individualized, and we can all learn from each other. In pairs, have students interview one another, asking the following questions:
- What is a new responsibility you've been given this year by your parents or family members?
- What is something you are supposed to ask for help with at home or at school that you'd like to try on your own?
- When you are an adult, what is something you think you'll do completely independently that you now need help with?
- When you are an adult, what is something you will still need help with because it isn't likely to be something you can do on your own?

Based on the answers to the questions, students will write about their partner's current and future sense of self-reliance.

☐ Monday:

Read the thought for the week. What did President Lincoln mean? Why isn't it helpful to do something for someone else that he or she could do on his or her own?

☐ Tuesday:

As young people grow up, they become more and more self-reliant. What is something that was once done for you that you now do for yourself? Write a short paragraph about that task and how you became self-reliant in that way.

☐ Wednesday:

What is something that others help you with now, but you know you'll eventually be able to do independently? Describe that task and the steps you'll need to take to become self-reliant in completing it.

☐ Thursday:

One step to becoming self-reliant is understanding when you still need help with a task or activity. Have you ever had the experience of beginning something independently and then realizing you needed help to finish it? Write about that experience and why it was important to ask for help.

☐ Friday:

Reflection – Reflect on this week's character study by responding to the following in at least one paragraph:

As I grow older, it is important that I become more self-reliant because…

WEEK TWENTY-THREE

Word of the Week:

Acceptance

Definition: Agreeing with or believing in an idea, opinion, explanation, or situation.

 **Thought for the Week:** "Acceptance doesn't mean giving up; it means understanding that something is the way it is and that there's got to be a way through it." (Michael J. Fox)

Class Activity:
Explain to students that accepting situations or conditions that cannot be changed does not mean being unhappy or giving up. As a class, brainstorm a list of conditions or situations in school that cannot be changed. Then, in pairs, have students write a short narrative about a positive aspect of one of those situations and how accepting it can lead to positive attitudes about other situations.

☐ Monday:

Read the thought for the week. What is the difference between giving up and accepting a situation?

☐ Tuesday:

Self-acceptance is very important to developing strong self-esteem. It is important to understand that there are things about yourself that you cannot change or control. Make a two-column chart. In the first column, list all the things about yourself that you can control. In the second column, list the things you cannot control.

☐ Wednesday:

Look at the chart you made yesterday. Choose one item from the column of things you cannot control. Do you accept that aspect of yourself? If not, what can you do to be more accepting of yourself?

☐ Thursday:

Look at the chart you made on Tuesday. Choose an attribute from the column of things you cannot control. Is this something that applies to others as well? Why is it important to understand that others must also deal with acceptance of situations or conditions they cannot control?

☐ Friday:

Reflection – Reflect on this week's character study by responding to the following in at least one paragraph:

> *Learning to accept that some things about myself and others cannot be changed is important because…*

WEEK TWENTY-FOUR

Word of the Week:

Accountability

Definition: The act of taking responsibility for your actions and behaviors.

 **Thought for the Week:** "It is wrong and immoral to seek to escape the consequences of one's acts." (Mahatma Gandhi)

Class Activity:
Scavenger Hunt – Make a list of words that describe things around the classroom (up to twenty, depending on the ages of students). Distribute one list to each group of four students. Students will divide up the items among themselves so that each person in the group is accountable for specific items. Students may not help find things that are not on their list. When you say "Go!" students will move around the room, gathering the items. Then they will return to their group and check off all of the items on the list they were able to find. The group that finds the most items wins a small prize. When the activity is done, ask students to reflect on how they felt accountable to their groups.

□ Monday:

Read the thought for the week. Why can it sometimes be difficult or unpleasant to accept the consequences of one's actions?

□ Tuesday:

Sometimes people do things without considering the consequences to themselves and to others. In those cases, should people be held accountable for their actions? Why or why not?

□ Wednesday:

Are there situations in which someone is too young or too inexperienced to be held accountable for his or her actions? Explain your answer.

□ Thursday:

In society, specific people are accountable for different aspects of our community. Make a list of public safety or environmental issues and explain who is accountable. For example, who is accountable for ensuring that roads are safe and well maintained?

□ Friday:

Reflection – Reflect on this week's character study by responding to the following in at least one paragraph:

Learning to be accountable for my own actions and behaviors is important because…

WEEK TWENTY-FIVE

Word of the Week:

 Courtesy

Definition: Showing respect and consideration of others.

 **Thought for the Week:** No one is too big to be courteous, but some are too small.

Class Activity:

Classroom Guidelines for Courteous Behavior – As a class, brainstorm a list of rules or procedures that reflect courteous behavior. When the list is complete, have students each write a short paragraph explaining how following these guidelines will make the classroom more pleasant for everyone.

☐ Monday:

Read the thought for the week. What does it mean to be too small to be courteous? What is the speaker saying about treating others with courtesy?

☐ Tuesday:

One way to be courteous is to have polite manners at meals. Explain how courteous people behave at the table and why those behaviors are courteous.

☐ Wednesday:

Some people make a habit of saying "please" and "thank you," while others don't use those words very often. Why is it important to be courteous when asking for something and to say thank you when you've received it?

☐ Thursday:

Write a dialogue or short play with at least two people in which one person is courteous, while the other is not. Choose one of the following situations or make up one of your own:

- Someone is playing with a toy, and another person would like to use it.
- One person cuts in front of another in line.
- One person wants to interrupt a conversation another person is having on the phone to ask a question.

☐ Friday:

Reflection – Reflect on this week's character study by responding to the following in at least one paragraph:

Being courteous makes the classroom and school community stronger because…

WEEK TWENTY-SIX

Word of the Week:

Empowerment

Definition: Making informed decisions and choices about one's own life.

 **Thought for the Week:** "Whether you say you can't, or you say you can, you're right." (Walt Disney)

Class Activity:
Writing "I Can..." Poems– Students will write poems in which the first line begins with "I can..." Based on the age group and your preference, students will write rhyming or free verse poems that celebrate what they can do currently with the skills they have. After sharing their poems with the class, students will return to their desks and revisit the poems, changing "I can" to "I will."

Monday:
Read the thought for the week. What does Mr. Disney mean about the power of what we tell ourselves?

Tuesday:
People feel empowered when they have an opportunity to share their opinions. What is one situation in which you'd like the opportunity to share your opinion? Explain how doing so would give you more control over your own choices.

Wednesday:
A good way to become empowered is to work toward something meaningful. In a paragraph, explain what success means to you. How are you empowered to achieve success?

Thursday:
Empowered people take action—they use their power to make changes. What action will you take this week to make a change that has a positive impact on you?

Friday:
Reflection – Reflect on this week's character study by responding to the following in at least one paragraph:

To become empowered, I must do the following things…

WEEK TWENTY-SEVEN

Word of the Week:

Forgiveness

Definition: To let go of feelings of resentment toward someone you believe has done something wrong.

 **Thought for the Week:** When you forgive, you don't change the past, but you certainly change the future.

Class Activity:

Place students in groups of three or more. Have each group write a community story about forgiveness that begins with one of the first lines below. Each student will write one sentence and then pass the story to the next student in the group. When five or ten minutes are left, let students know that it's time to wrap up the story. Then have students share stories.

- The last time I played basketball with Tommy, he pushed me down.
- I was really looking forward to going to the beach, but now we can't go.
- My best friend forgot my birthday!
- My brother's new puppy chewed up my favorite shoes.

☐ Monday:

Read the thought for the week. Why does forgiving someone for what he or she has done in the past change the future of a relationship between two people?

☐ Tuesday:

What is the difference between forgetting something that has happened and forgiving someone for something that has happened? Is it necessary to forget in order to forgive?

☐ Wednesday:

Holding on to resentment can have a negative impact on a person's attitude and outlook. Explain why it might benefit someone to let go of feelings of resentment and forgive someone for a mistake.

☐ Thursday:

Write a dialogue or short play that illustrates forgiveness in one of the following situations:

- One of your siblings borrowed your bicycle without your permission, and now it has a flat tire.
- Your parent agreed to take you to a movie on Saturday but instead had to go to work.
- While you were playing, a friend accidentally kicked you, causing a painful bruise.

☐ Friday:

Reflection – Reflect on this week's character study by responding to the following in at least one paragraph:

Practicing forgiveness benefits me and others because…

WEEK TWENTY-EIGHT

Word of the Week:

Honorable

Definition: Showing honesty, respect, and good moral character. Being fair and worthy of respect.

Thought for the Week: When you are faced with a choice, do the honorable thing, even if it doesn't seem to be the choice that will benefit you most.

Class Activity:

Create an Honor Board – With students, brainstorm a list of traits or behaviors that the class feels are honorable. Put every student's name on the board along with spaces for up to ten check marks. When a student observes another student demonstrating one of the traits the class has determined is honorable, he or she will submit an honor nomination to you. The nomination must include a clear explanation of what the student has done and why it is honorable. Review the nomination and add a check mark next to the student's name. Whenever a student reaches ten check marks, present him or her with a certificate of honor acknowledging his or her strong character.

□ Monday:

Read the thought for the week. What is an example of a situation in which the honorable choice would not seem to benefit you as much as a dishonorable choice?

□ Tuesday:

Academic dishonesty, such as cheating on a test or copying information from another student or the Internet, may seem like a quick solution to getting a good grade. Explain why cheating and copying are not honorable activities.

□ Wednesday:

Many public figures are considered honorable because of their actions or good deeds. Who is a famous person you consider honorable? Why do you think that person is honorable?

□ Thursday:

People learn to behave in a way that is honorable in part from being a part of a community that values honorable traits. How are you modeling an honorable character for others in your community? Explain one example of a situation in which you behaved honorably.

□ Friday:

Reflection – Reflect on this week's character study by responding to the following in at least one paragraph:

It benefits me and my community when I demonstrate an honorable character because…

WEEK TWENTY-NINE

Word of the Week:

Initiative

Definition: The ability to act independently or take charge of a situation.

 **Thought for the Week:** "The best way to not feel hopeless is to get up and do something." (Barack Obama)

Class Activity:

Finding a Mentor – Have each student write his or her name on a sheet of paper and, below it, describe something he or she is very good at doing. Then have students review the sheets and choose a mentor from within the class who can give them tips to improve in that area. After conferencing with their mentors, students will write about what they've learned and how it will help them improve.

☐ Monday:
Read the thought for the week. How is President Obama's quote related to the definition of initiative?

☐ Tuesday:
What is something that is very important to your success, but you're not as good at as you'd like to be? Write a plan to improve in that area and begin to work on the plan immediately.

☐ Wednesday:
What if? Think about what you'd like to see change in your own life or in your community. Make a list of "What if…" statements that reflect those changes.

☐ Thursday:
It can be easy to procrastinate, especially when the task isn't something you'd like to do. Explain what you are procrastinating about now and how you will take initiative and complete the task.

☐ Friday:
Reflection – Reflect on this week's character study by responding to the following in at least one paragraph:

> *Taking initiative can benefit me throughout my life because…*

WEEK THIRTY

Word of the Week:

Leadership

Definition: The ability to provide appropriate guidance and direction to others.

 **Thought for the Week:** A leader is one who knows the way, goes the way, and shows the way.

Class Activity:

Sharing Leadership – Over the course of several weeks, give students the opportunity to lead a class discussion. With the class, discuss the qualities they would most appreciate in a discussion leader. Then, each day, assign one student to be a discussion leader on one topic being covered in class. The student will determine the discussion questions, call on others, and decide when the discussion has ended. After each student's turn, discuss that student's leadership strengths.

☐ Monday:
Read the thought for the week. What is the difference between knowing the way, going the way, and showing the way?

☐ Tuesday:
Society relies on strong leaders in government, education, science, and other areas. Name an important leader from the past or present and explain what makes or made this person an effective leader.

☐ Wednesday:
A good leader empowers others. Why is it important for a leader to let others have power in a group or organization?

☐ Thursday:
Strong leaders are empathetic—they listen to and understand the emotions of those they lead. Why is empathy important in a leader? Isn't it just as important for a leader to have a strong sense of what should be done and just do it? Why or why not?

☐ Friday:
Reflection – Reflect on this week's character study by responding to the following in at least one paragraph:

Good leaders are…

WEEK THIRTY-ONE

Word of the Week:

Motivation

Definition: The basic desire or willingness to do something.

 **Thought for the Week:** Ability is what you're capable of doing. Motivation determines what you actually accomplish.

Class Activity:

Suggestion Apples – Since students are motivated by situations in which they feel they have some input, allow students to make suggestions about classroom activities or areas of study. Your responses don't need to be lengthy lessons. Rather, student interests can be incorporated into other lessons. For example, if a student wants to learn about dinosaurs, incorporate some information about dinosaurs into word problems during math.

Hand each student a cutout of an apple. Ask him or her to write down something he or she would like to learn. Put the apples up on half a bulletin board. Once you have covered the material on each apple, move it to the other side.

☐ Monday:

Read the thought for the week. What is the difference between ability and motivation? Is it important to have both? Why or why not?

☐ Tuesday:

People often feel motivated when they are in control of a situation and its outcomes. Write about something in your school experience that you don't feel you have control of. How can you earn more control of the situation, and how will that lead to you being more motivated?

☐ Wednesday:

Some people are motivated by competition with others. Why does competition motivate people? Are you motivated by competition? Why or why not?

☐ Thursday:

Some people feel motivated when they work with another student. Why does working with someone else motivate some people? Does it motivate you? Why or why not?

☐ Friday:

Reflection – Reflect on this week's character study by responding to the following in at least one paragraph:

Some things that motivate me are...

WEEK THIRTY-TWO

Word of the Week:

Patience

Definition: The ability to tolerate a delay, trouble, or inconvenience without becoming angry.

Thought for the Week: Have patience. All things are difficult before they become easy.

Class Activity:

Explain to students that growing a plant from a seed requires patience. With your help, have student plant flower seeds in a small container of soil. Have them place the containers on the windowsill and water them regularly as they wait for the seeds to sprout. Then, as a class, have students write a patience journal reflecting on their feelings each day as they wait for the seeds to sprout.

☐ Monday:

Read the thought for the week. What is an example of something in your experience that was difficult before it was easy? How did having patience benefit you?

☐ Tuesday:

Some professions require patience. For example, a farmer must be patient while his or her crops grow. Describe another profession that requires patience and why being impatient would negatively impact someone's success in that field.

☐ Wednesday:

There are certainly times in your life when you must practice patience, for example, when you have to wait in a line or wait your turn to do something. What is one strategy you can use to remain calm, even if you are eager to have your turn?

☐ Thursday:

Have you ever lost your temper or become impatient with a situation or another person? Describe that situation and how, now that you've had an opportunity to reflect, you might have changed your behavior or reaction.

☐ Friday:

Reflection – Reflect on this week's character study by responding to the following in at least one paragraph:

Being patient benefits me and benefits those around me because...

WEEK THIRTY-THREE

Word of the Week:

Perseverance

Definition: Not giving up, regardless of obstacles or challenges.

 **Thought for the Week:** "Perseverance is failing 19 times and succeeding the 20th." (Julie Andrews)

Class Activity:

In pairs or groups of three, have students choose one of the famous people below and use the Internet or other resources to research the person's success. Then have students create a poster that shows how the person's perseverance led to success. Students will present their posters to the class. Hang the posters around the classroom to inspire others.

- Walt Disney
- Albert Einstein
- Thomas Edison
- Princess Diana
- Oprah Winfrey
- Theodor Seuss Giesel (Dr. Seuss)
- Harriet Beecher Stowe
- Amelia Earhart
- J.K. Rowling
- Julie Andrews
- Charles Schultz
- Steven Spielberg

☐ **Monday:**

Read the thought for the week. Julie Andrews enjoyed a very successful acting and singing career before retiring. How might perseverance have been important to her success?

☐ **Tuesday:**

It can be easy to celebrate success without realizing the hard work that led to that success. Think about a recent time when you were successful. Perhaps you did well on a test, won at a sport, or performed well in a concert or recital. How did perseverance play a role in that success?

☐ **Wednesday:**

Thomas Edison experienced failure more than a thousand times before he invented a light bulb that worked. Explain how our lives would be different if Mr. Edison did not have perseverance.

☐ **Thursday:**

What is one personal goal of yours that will require perseverance? How will you stay motivated if, like Mr. Edison, you don't experience immediate success?

☐ **Friday:**

Reflection – Reflect on this week's character study by responding to the following in at least one paragraph:

Perseverance will help me achieve my personal goals because…

WEEK THIRTY-FOUR

Word of the Week:

Resilience

Definition: The ability to recover quickly from difficulties or challenges.

 **Thought for the Week:** Persistence and resilience only come from having the experience of working through difficult problems.

Class Activity:

Have students watch a movie that demonstrates a character who is resilient. Some suggests include:

- The Goonies
- The Mighty Ducks
- Soul Surfer
- Apollo 13

(Review for appropriateness for the age group.)

Students will choose one character from the movie and explain how the character showed resilience in the face of a challenge or problem that was difficult to overcome.

☐ Monday:

Read the thought for the week. Do you think the author considers working through a tough problem a good experience? Why or why not?

☐ Tuesday:

Everyone faces difficult situations in life. One strategy that will help build resilience, or the ability to get through a difficulty, is to know who you can turn to for help. Who can you turn to when you face a difficult situation? How can that person help you?

☐ Wednesday:

Resilient people try new things and don't give up when they don't immediately succeed. What is something you've tried and had to work hard to succeed at? It could be a sport, a new skill, or even a game. What made you stay positive and try again?

☐ Thursday:

Resilient people can see the positive in any experience, even if they are not immediately successful. Consider one of the following situations or one of your own. What would be a positive outcome, even if you were not immediately successful?

- You wrote a story for a local competition, but your story did not win.
- You hoped to try out for a sports team, but on the day of the tryouts your family had an emergency and you could not attend.
- You looked forward to receiving a new game, but when it finally arrived it was defective and didn't work.
- You studied for a test, but you didn't earn a very high grade.

☐ Friday:

Reflection – Reflect on this week's character study by responding to the following in at least one paragraph:

It is important to be resilient in the face of difficulty because…

WEEK THIRTY-FIVE

Word of the Week:

 **Respect**

Definition: A feeling of admiration for someone or something that is good, valuable, or important.

 **Thought for the Week:** "Everyone should be respected as an individual." (Albert Einstein)

Class Activity:

In groups of three or more, have students make a Respect banner to hang in the classroom or school. It can be made from cardboard, butcher paper, or another material. In the middle of the banner, students should write the word RESPECT in large capital letters. All around the word, in smaller letters, they should write examples of how to show respect in school.

☐ Monday:

Read the thought for the week. What does Mr. Einstein mean? Why is every individual worthy of respect or admiration?

☐ Tuesday:

Make a list of synonyms for the word respect. Choose three and use them in sentences about your school or classroom.

☐ Wednesday:

Explain why it is important to respect other people's property.

☐ Thursday:

How do you show respect to your parents and other family members? Write about a situation in which you were respectful toward another member of your family.

☐ Friday:

Reflection – Reflect on this week's character study by responding to the following in at least one paragraph:

It is important to be respectful of others because…

WEEK THIRTY-SIX

Word of the Week:

Sportsmanship

Definition: Playing fair, following the rules of the game, respecting the judgment of officials, and treating all players—even opponents—with respect.

 **Thought for the Week:** Sportsmanship is knowing that it is a game, that we are only as good as our opponents, and whether we win or lose, to always give 100 percent.

Class Activity:

In groups of three or more, have students write a dialogue or short play in which one character shows good sportsmanship and another shows poor sportsmanship. Have students choose one of the following situations or make one up themselves. Have groups perform their play for the class.

- An official has made a call that you disagree with that benefits the opposing team.
- After several seasons of losing to a team, your team has finally won.
- A player on your team makes an error on the field that allows the opposing team to score.
- A player on the opposing team makes an error that allows you to score.

☐ Monday:
Read the thought for the week. What does it mean to say "We are only as good as our opponents?"

☐ Tuesday:
Showing good sportsmanship means avoiding arguments with coaches, officials, or opponents. If you disagree with an official or coach, what can you do to resolve the issue and still be a good sport?

☐ Wednesday:
On a team, everyone shares in the responsibility of playing a game. Why should stronger players support less talented players?

☐ Thursday:
In any game, it is fair to assume that the opposing team has worked as hard as your own team. How can you respect the other team's effort, regardless of whether you win or lose the game?

☐ Friday:
Reflection – Reflect on this week's character study by responding to the following in at least one paragraph:

It's important to demonstrate good sportsmanship because…

Author | Erainna Winnett

Erainna was born and raised in central Louisiana. The oldest of five children she always yearned to be a teacher and forced her siblings to play school year round. Naturally, she graduated with a teaching degree in 1995 and earned her master's degree in 2000. Five years later she earned her education specialist degree in early childhood education. After fifteen years in the classroom, she moved to the role of school counselor and has never been happier.

While serving as school counselor at an elementary school in northeast Texas, she frequently uses children's books as therapy to help her students heal, learn, and grow. Ideas for her books come from the students she works with on a daily basis. Her goal, as an author, is to touch the hearts of children, one story at a time. Erainna lives on a 300 acre cattle ranch near the Red River with her husband, two daughters, three dogs, two horses, and one ill-tempered cat.

To see more books by Erainna, please visit her counseling website counselingwithheart.com.

Made in the USA
Lexington, KY
21 August 2014